Eduard Wagner 2017

Preface

You can see it how you want: Are these memoirs or is it just a sequence of events in my life. I would like to say that at the time I had experienced this, I believed that this was correct. I hardly had any advice from relatives or friends as to whether that was the right thing to do or not. But it was always a question of whether I would have taken this into account. Of course, in the course of the following pages there are always places where I am on the verge of legality. But since these were sometimes ago and I personally stand by what I did or didn't do then, I don't see any problems if these consequences arise. Whether this is a fulfilled or happy life is not up to me, but to the reader, but I will draw a conclusion in the end.

© 2021 Eduard Wagner
Herstellung und Verlag: BoD – Books on Demand, Norderstedt
ISBN: 9783755756484

Family 1970

December 1959 parental home

At the end of 1959 I saw the light of day in Vienna, although I was there but can hardly remember it. Came as the second born, my brother was already 6 years old in a Danube Swabian family. To explain my origins: At the end of the Second World War, my parents were expelled from what is now Serbia by partisans at gunpoint and their lives were threatened. Since they belonged to the group of ethnic Germans (Danube Swabians), their mother tongue was German, which means that they could also speak Serbo-Croatian. Their ancestors were currently settled by Prinz Eugen in what was then Yugoslavia in order to strengthen the infrastructure there, which they succeeded in doing. In the turmoil of World War II, they were then driven out by partisans from both the north and the south with the threat of their lives. By this time, they had achieved prosperity and reputation, where there was no hostility whatsoever between the Yugoslavs living there and the German-speaking population. My parents and their families were welcomed in 1944 with the words: What are you doing there? Why do you speak German so well? Sneak your way home. Back then it was just the reception of "foreigners". One can no longer imagine today. Well back to me. Had an easy childhood, at least until I was 10 years old. My father pursued his trade, which he had already learned in Serbia, and my mother was, as was still the custom back then, a housewife. As far as my parents' means allowed, I got everything from toys to bicycles and the like. In the summer I went to a guesthouse in southern Lower Austria every year with my brother and my mother for two to three weeks. My father, since he had to work during the week for financial reasons, came to us on Friday by moped and stayed until Sunday. It should be noted that my father only got his driver's license in 1972. At that time, I also got to know a family who lived near the pension. There were two daughters in this one, one five years younger and the other one year older. Means the older one has already met me with diapers.

September 1966 school

Start of my school career. In elementary school I was in an all-boys class. A graduate of the then Pädag introduced herself as a teacher. She was about 25 years old and a beautiful woman as far as I could tell at that age. I can still remember an anecdote that shocked me quite a bit at the time. At the beginning of my school days, I came to my mother and told her the following: You, mother, the teacher painted her fingers bright red. How can you do something like that? The background was that teacher Ulrike had only painted her fingernails, which was not yet commonplace for me at the time. I think my mother turned to the side at the time and probably had to smile, then explained to me what that was all about. Well, I graduated from elementary school with very good grades, apart from painting and drawing. But I also had respect for the "woman teacher", who punished offenses with "standing in the corner". The way to school, back then everything on foot, was always a challenge, because there were always one, two or three school colleagues with whom you could juggle on the sidewalk.

September 1970 high school After I kept dreaming of the dream job "doctor" at this age and my primary school certificate was accordingly, my parents registered me in the neighboring district in the high school. In 1969, my father had returned his trade license for the repair of soda water bottles because it was no longer profitable and he subsequently turned to a new job, namely selling daily newspapers. That means he sold the largest newspaper in our country as a colporteur in the evening until about 11 p.m. on a stand. Since this was halfway profitable, my mother also started selling newspapers. With this they could save themselves a lot of money over the years, both of us, that is my brother and I, well-being was not neglected. Well, now I was in the first grade of the humanistic high school. On Mondays there was always math and English one after the other. Well, that went halfway for a while, but after a while I got sick and my parents wrote me a confirmation that I was sick. But since the teaching staff did not take this paper from me, I kept it. Now Monday with English and math became more and more repugnant to me, so I got the idea to go "blue" on one or the other Monday and not go to school. I then produced the confirmation that I was sick myself with my parents' signature. Since it was mostly the same illnesses and the signature was no longer the best, it happened as it had to. Suddenly my parents received a summons to come to school. Of course, they were asked about my missing days and the resulting grades and they were accordingly surprised or disappointed in me. The consequence of this was that the school condemned me to a "cataclysm" (4 hours of writing punishment alone in school). To the best of my knowledge, this type of punishment no longer exists today. Finally, the school year ended with two fives. So that means I had to repeat the 1st class, as it was then still required.

September 1971 boarding school

After this decisive event for me, the family council met in the form of my parents and my seventeen-year-old brother. It would have to be sent in advance that my father was in a German-speaking boarding school for a few years during his school days in Serbia. Thus, advice was given as to which school I should continue to go to. Since, of course, at the age of 11 I had no idea or only limited what was in store for me, I had to accept the decision of the family council. Since I was baptized Protestant from birth, my registration at Catholic boarding schools, such as school brothers in Strebersdorf, was not accepted. This decision meant that I went to a boarding school in the 13th district, which also included a humanistic grammar school. I quarreled with this decision on the part of my parents for a long time, because I was more or less locked up there from Sunday evening to Saturday noon. If I had "broken" something during the week, there was of course no outcome on the weekend either. Fortunately, that was rarely the case in the 13th district. One thing was interesting in this house, because the head of this institution was the grandson of Adalbert Stifter (his name was the same). This director was an avid pipe smoker, where the smoke could be smelled all over the building and, of increasing intensity, we knew that danger was imminent. I spent 3 years at Himmelhof, that's how the boarding school there was named. Then I moved to the boarding school of the same name in the 2nd district with the same tutor Franz. But the customs there were the same as in the 13th district. That means, if there were misconduct on my part during the week, I was involuntarily allowed to spend the weekend with punishment in the boarding school. Since the supervision there was not very great and I have of course also gotten older, there were often weekends in the boarding school. At that time, at the age of 13, I made the acquaintance of cigarettes, which also resulted in me being forced to stay in the home. This friendship with nicotine has stayed with me to this day. The whole thing went reasonably well up to 4th grade and then we got a Carinthian teacher in biology who had just finished her studies. For us students between the ages of 14 and 15, of course, she was a challenge in terms of puberty, because she was a pretty woman with a corresponding figure. So, I let myself be carried away to one statement during the lesson that earned me the worst grade of conduct. In addition, I also collected the worst grades in various objects, so that I had to repeat the 4th grade. This had succeeded and so, since this was no longer taught in the house, I had to go to the 5th grade of the humanistic grammar school in the neighboring district. Since I still wanted to become a doctor, I assumed I would use ancient Greek, as I also liked the Latin language very much. It was interesting at the time that I ended up in a mixed class for the first time, but there were only 6 girls and the rest of the boys. In the first semester I was still a little eager to learn, but since I didn't like ancient Greek at all, the grades looked accordingly. It didn't stop with this subject alone and so I would have had to repeat the class, only that was no longer possible at the time. So, my parents decided, since I was now 17 years old, that I would start an apprenticeship. When I was about 16, when I was still in boarding school, I was approached by Ernst, who was the son of a friend of my mother's, whether I might not want to go to folk dances every Friday evening. That was of course a difficult undertaking at the boarding school, as it was not always the case that going out from there. In the end, I was finally allowed to go out on Friday from 6pm to 10pm. The folk dancing took place in the home of the Danube Swabians in the 3rd district. When I first got there, I found about 30 young men and women, of which I was one of the youngest. A native Danube Swabian introduced himself to me as the leader, who rehearsed the folk dances with us. But since I was a decidedly anti-talent when it came to dancing, this man also had his difficulties teaching me that. I can still remember an episode in which the supervisor took my thigh in his hand because I did not understand the sequence of an alternating step. Probably nothing has changed about that to this day. On these evenings we studied folk dances with 8 to 10 couples, which we then performed in the ball season in January and February. In the course of time, a group of people of the same age developed who went bowling twice a week in the Vienna Prater. This means training once a week and championship on Friday. Since we had a sponsor, a shipping company, that didn't cost us too much. Around 1982 7 men and women then sailed with this company on a 10-man sailing ship from Split to Dubrovnik in the summer. Every day that week we went to an island, took a break and then drove on. It was a wonderful experience

August 1972 weekend house

After my father's career change in 1969 was successful in terms of savings, they were able to save themselves quite a bit of money. Now my parents went looking for a small weekend house in Lower Austria. They found what they were looking for in the southern Vienna Basin in a municipality with around 10,000 inhabitants. The first sight struck my parents as a bargain, but they couldn't imagine what came next. For me as a 12-year-old it was of course a pleasure, because there were plenty of fruit trees and bushes on the property that I was allowed to burn after sawing off, so that the building from 1930 could also be seen. I can remember that after a while the burning bothered the neighbors a bit, at that time this was still allowed. But yes, we were "Viennese" who came to Lower Austria to expand. Well, the trees and bushes were eliminated and you could see the house. It had the disadvantage that it had not been used for years and was therefore in a desolate condition with a floor and an attic. When I had burned everything, I took my bike and explored the area with the mountains that belonged to it and had to drive past a workers' settlement again and again. One day a guy who was just there asked me if I could get off my bike and sit down with him. I did as he had asked and sat down with him. Then more boys came along and an interesting conversation developed. From this meeting a friendship developed for at least ten years and we did something different every weekend. Only over the years did the partners join, each of these friends moved somewhere else in Lower Austria and the friendships dissolved.

House after renovation

1972 first kiss

Since my parents always wanted to go on vacation in the summer, they asked the evangelical church in Vienna that the whole family had the same faith. This resulted in holidays with the whole family in Styria. We weren't the only family there, there were about 50 people. We did every day with all the excursions and hikes which were always nice. One day, we came back from an excursion a little earlier, Angela spoke to me, she was about a year younger than me. She said that she had discovered a hornet's nest in the attic of the house where we lived and that she was afraid to look at it again alone, whether I should come with you. Well, why not, nothing can happen. When we stood in front of this nest, she suddenly turned around and kissed me on the lips. I was horrified, only my mother was allowed to do that and no one else was allowed to do it. But I kept it to myself anyway.

Winter 1975 sale

Since my brother wanted to earn something in addition to his salary as a bank clerk, he drove from one restaurant to another in the 10th district and sold the largest daily newspaper there. But since we were one heart and one soul until he was about 20, he said I could sell newspapers and buy my pocket money. To do this, I was standing in a pedestrian zone in the 10th district wearing a yellow jacket and praising my newspapers. We then settled the accounts for the 10 to 15 newspapers in the evening. Wasn't very profitable, but, as I said, my pocket money was increased.

September 1977 apprenticeship

My father knew the HR manager of a large grocery wholesaler and producer in the 16th district, which was well-known at the time, and so I started an apprenticeship as an office clerk. The first thing I did was work in wholesale accounting. I found four men there aged 50 and over there. The department head for this was an authorized signatory. But since I had just come out of boarding school before, I enjoyed my regained freedom. This manifested itself in the fact that I was not so strict about getting a night's sleep in my free time. That means, now that I had a friend in Vienna by the name of Ernst, we left almost every evening in the evening. Of course, going home was late. So, my work performance on the following day was accordingly. The general manager, to whom I was sitting with my back, tapped the table again and again with the ballpoint pen so that I could continue working. In the course of time, however, the work of only adding 100 to 200 delivery notes in a whole day became too boring for me and so I decided to speak to my boss about whether I could be transferred to another department in the company. My request was granted and I was transferred to the tea department. There I met a young dispatcher and his boss was an authorized signatory. Here I didn't learn too much about the office clerk, but the old manager taught me a lot about tea. So, I had to set up the tea tasting every morning, which went through a very special ritual: So, I started by setting up at least 10 bowls of hot water and then only allowed exactly 2 grams of tea to be added. Then the gentleman went through and took a sip of each bowl, keeping it in his mouth and letting it run over his taste buds. With this handling he was able to determine the quality of this tea and then the corresponding quantity was ordered. In the course of my work in this department, an automatic plant for the production of tea bags was added, which fascinated me very much, because on one side the tea delivered was in large boxes and at the end the finished 20-25 tea bags came out packed. But since what I could learn was limited, I wanted to go back to a new department and so I came to the fresh produce department when I was about 18 years old. From there, the fruit and vegetable deliveries for the 250 branches were prepared daily. To do this, the individual shops had to take orders by telephone every day, of course. Since I had now reached the age where I was allowed to work overtime according to the Youth Protection Act, I signed up for Sunday services, which were appropriately remunerated. My colleagues were pretty much my age, so friendships soon formed. So, every now and then we went to have a drink after our Sunday work, until someone said he had something with him that could only be consumed in closed rooms. Naive as I was back then, we went into an apartment and sat on the floor for lack of seats. Suddenly the said colleague took a cigarette out of his pocket, lit it and passed it on. Unsuspecting, I, like the others, attracted this supposed cigarette. Then when it was smoked out, I was informed that this was a joint. My summary of it was good, my gullibility and above all, I hadn't felt anything, so the matter was settled for me and I never touched anything like that again.

September 1978 First apartment

After my brother had said at the age of about 21 that he would no longer have a wife and that he already had his own apartment, I got the small apartment of around 35 square meters in the same house where my parents lived in Vienna. At this time, however, also began where I had to struggle for about 30 years. On the one hand, I had one-time friends over the weekend in Lower Austria and a friend in Vienna. With the latter I went out almost every day during the week, and so it happened that we didn't do a lot of different things. We then mostly went to bars where you could play cards. But since this got a bit boring over time, we decided to play for money. But that wasn't fulfilling either, and so we saw machines in local machines where you could insert money and win. At that time, they were called one-armed bandits that could be found all over Austria. Yes, in the beginning there were always smaller or larger profits, but in the course of time it was of course a deficit. Above all, I discovered that such devices were also available in Lower Austria. And so, my addiction began, certainly not right away, but in the course of time I had crossed a line that I was not aware of.

May 1978 color blindness

At that time, I had to go to the Austrian Armed Forces for drafting. At that time, I had no health complaints, but then a card with different colored dots was presented to me and I was asked to read a number and a letter from it. But I couldn't do this, even if I looked at the maps from different angles. In other words, it was found that I am color-blind, namely red-green-blind. However, the Commission has determined that I would be fully qualified. Half a year later I wanted to get my motorbike and car driver's license with my father. To do this, however, I also had to endure a test. Among other things, I was presented with another color card from which I could not read anything again. Then they said that I would have to undergo further examinations, including a reaction test at the respective board of trustees and a psychological test in the 3rd district. This psychological test had about 20 pages and it was tedious to fill out because I did not make sense of it. My argument, which I also expressed, was that I am fully qualified and I am not allowed to have a driver's license, well then, I'll just shoot you because I can't decide between red and green. As far as I know, only the red at the traffic light is always in the same place. I finally got the driver's license for at least a car, I gave up the one for motorcycles, even though I had 2 mopeds when I was 16 and 17, and I never had any accidents with them.

October 1980 Federal Army

At the beginning of October, I did my military service with the Austrian Armed Forces in the Martinek barracks (pension?). The first six weeks were basic training and also exhausting. When it was my birthday at the beginning of December, I was on call, of all things, and that on a public holiday. This means that around 15 people had been given 20 rounds of live ammunition for each by the guard on duty. Now I had to sit at the table and wait for an order to come, say to walk around the barracks. I don't know how, but suddenly there was a 2-liter bottle with white wine on the table and my comrades cheered me for my birthday. Yes, but unfortunately it wasn't the only bottle we consumed. That means during the next round of checks in the barracks area the path got narrower and narrower and at the end I had to unload my rifle with 20 rounds of live ammunition in the loopholes. I hadn't managed to do this myself, a comrade helped me. The whole thing remained unpunished except for a compulsory report with the following admonition. After the first six weeks, I was assigned to the press officer's office. This major was there in the morning, but then left the office and came back an hour before the end of work. My job there was to look for reports about the sovereign in the various daily newspapers. It wasn't a time-consuming task, it was completed pretty quickly. So, I was able to catch up on what I had very little during the night, namely sleep. When I moved in in October, I was 65 kilos divided over my length. In the area of the barracks, I got to know Baden wine because I hadn't known it before. When I disarmed after 8 months, I weighed not 65, but 72 kilos, which I had not exceeded until today.

September 1980 profession

I had successfully completed my apprenticeship as an office clerk, the military service less successfully, and so I thought to myself how to go on. Now I became interested in evening courses and started an accountant course, which soon turned out to be wrong for me. So, I found that computers had a future and from 1980 to 1981 I took programming courses at WIFI Vienna, which went every evening from 6 p.m. to 10 p.m. I completed this with exams at least in Pascal, in Cobol I did not pass. With the certificates I meant I had better chances on the job market and at the end of August 1981 I quit my job at the grocery wholesaler. I immediately had a job again as an office clerk in a company that manufactured pipes and switch boxes, which was located in the 5th district. After about a year we moved to the 11th district, where the factory of this company was also located. There I had a likable older business graduate who had tried again and again to inspire me. But when he retired, a woman graduate engineer came as his successor. This had the goal of making savings and so it came about that I was fired after two years and nine months. At that time there was still severance pay with at least two salaries, but only after three years with the company. So, I had to look around for a new job and found out about it in the daily newspapers. Then I found a job where the preselection was made in a test psychological institute. So, I came to this institute at the beginning of May 1984 and was presented with a bundle of 20 pages of tests to fill out. After making a few entries in this paper, I thought to myself that I had already held these sheets of paper in my hand. And that's exactly how it was, years earlier I had to take the same test to get a driver's license and that day to apply for a job. Sounds a bit strange. After evaluating my information, I was asked for an interview in the 8th district. The prerequisite for this position was that it was only a one-year parental leave substitute. There I had to account for the scholarship holders who worked at the research center in Lower Austria and also look after the bank book. But since the whole thing was a little too little challenge for me, I aimed at further tasks. These included finance, budget and asset accounting. The computer languages I had learned, which I had acquired years before, were not used because this was prevented by the existing "programmer". So, the first year of maternity leave came to an end and my boss at the time, with whom I now had a stone in the board, extended my contract without hesitation. But since the office in the 8th district was closed about a year after joining this company (semi-public), we had to move to Lower Austria. We had the opportunity to use the company bus from Vienna. But work didn't start until 8:30 a.m. and that was too late for me. So, I talked to a colleague that we would drive to work together with my 2nd car. In doing so, she contributed to the travel expenses. That means getting out of bed every working day at 6 a.m., driving 35 km out and 35 km back in the evening, whatever the weather. But since I valued this work in Lower Austria at all, I accepted that. The time that I spent there was not only professional, but also personally the experience-rich work that I had in my life, especially since I had learned a lot from it. In accounting, that was the name of the department where I worked, there were around 15 women and only 2 men, which initially affected me less. Over the years, however, I made friends with a colleague who worked two rooms away. She was about 2 years younger and pretty smart, lived near her work with her parents in a two-family house. As it had to come, it was, friendship became more. Most of the time I stayed at her home, but kept going back to my apartment in Vienna. Then one day she told me that she was pregnant with me. I was then about 26 years old and he saw it as my duty to propose to her because she accepted. We were already looking for a church or a registry office and more or less set a date for the wedding. In the company, of course, it was rumored in secret that something was going on that I didn't really like. However, since on her part it was only the statement of pregnancy and I couldn't see or hear anything else over the course of the months, I became skeptical whether this would be true. Now, in addition, the "pressure" of the colleagues became greater and greater. So, at the end of 1987 I decided to quit my position after three and a half years and let her take precedence in the company because her qualifications were less than mine. Of course, there was also no settlement of two salaries, since I had resigned myself. I checked the alleged pregnancy of my girlfriend at the time sometime later, but she was probably never pregnant. I was sorry for this position because I had learned a lot, even if the conditions weren't always the best.

January 1988 employed by father Since my father was 58 years old this year, I decided to start working for him as an office clerk, which means I was more or less self-employed at this point, because a father can't do too much for his son. Since I had bookkeeping in vocational school, we decided that we would do the bookkeeping ourselves. Our tax advisor only had the task of preparing the respective tax return or balance sheet and submitting it to the tax office. In 1989 the same tax advisor said that an amount of S 0.25 in the balance sheet was just a Mickey Mouse amount and was therefore irrelevant. So, we terminated our contract with him and for the following years I prepared the income tax returns and the resulting balance sheet myself. Of course, the only disadvantage of this was that I had no experience in this regard. So, in the following year I received a letter from the responsible tax office. When I opened it, I read a stipulation of 1.5 million schillings in arrears. Fortunately, I was sitting when I opened this letter. I made a comma mistake while filling out the relevant form. After about 4 to 5 appointments, I corrected that. During this time, I had around 100 colporteurs (customers) whom I had to deliver every day, very few had the time to come to our business premises in the 20th district. To explain a colporteur was a person who sold daily newspapers in the evening or in the morning with colored jackets in squares, train stations and streets. For me, they were always considered to be independent merchants. This means that they bought magazines from me, i.e. periodical printed works, at a certain discount and then sold them at a fixed end-of-sale price that is specified on each product. The disadvantage of this industry is that there is a 100 percent right of return. If a customer bought 10 pieces of a magazine from me and only sold 5 of them, he was able to return the remaining 5 pieces to me when the magazine was new and these were then offset against. Of course, I also had the right with my suppliers, such as wholesalers and publishers. The whole thing was of course associated with an enormous amount of time and, above all, with a precise control of the respective invoices. Thus, a 50-to-60-hour week was not the exception, but rather the rule.

September 1992 self-employment

My father was already 62 this year and I had to make a lot of arguments to him that he had finally started his retirement after 47 years of contribution. It wouldn't have got him very much financially. So, I took over this magazine wholesaler with two trade licenses, there was no other way back then. Means two memberships of the chamber division and, as a result, two fees for it. Then two to three years later a competitor appeared. This Mr. Robin got the opportunity to set up his own colportage from a smaller daily newspaper. In other words, he provided several foreign people with jackets and daily newspapers and distributed these people all over Vienna. In the course of time, however, I learned that this man did not give people the places for free, but rather demanded a deposit in 5 to 6-digit shilling amounts from each person and that even before a place was assigned to him. Since, as far as I know, this was only written very sparsely in writing, I already suspected at this point that this would go wrong at some point. Since this did not concern me very much, I let him rule. Then one day he came up to me and said that we could do counter-deals, which I had no objection to. I got magazines from some Viennese publishers on good terms and it wasn't very different with him. This went well for a while, he delivered to me, I to him and it was offset against. But one day, it wasn't a huge amount to get, the phone rang and Robin was on the line. He said that I still owed him something and that he wanted to claim it. That got me so furious that I said I renounced my request and didn't want to hear from him anymore. Yes, well, that was just my wish. He hired more and more Arabs, Pakistani and Indians and then finally went to my two main suppliers. The background to this is that when I started working in the magazine wholesale business, I spoke to these two suppliers to get the 4.9% higher discount. That means instead of 28.2% the higher one with 33.1% gross. My request for it remained unanswered even when I drove to the head office of one supplier in Salzburg, I had then achieved the discount increase about 10 years later. Mr. Robin went to these two suppliers with whatever and immediately had the higher discount, which connection was clear to me, but I will not give this one from me.

Business premises in the 20th district with father

November 1988

I was now 28 years old, my Lower Austrian friends had split up all over the federal state, partly for professional reasons, partly for reasons of partnership, and so I was on my own. Once again it was such a bland Saturday and then the idea occurred to me that there were two girls living there 30 kilometers away, whom I already knew from my childhood days when I spent the summer with my brother and mother in Lower Austria. So, I got in my car and drove to this town of 800 people. I found not only two girls, but 3. The friend of the older woman was visiting. After a short time, I made the suggestion that we could go dancing. The friend said she was tired and had to go home to her husband. So, I had the two left and after some time of make-up and styling, the time had come. We drove my car about 60 kilometers to the neighboring district, there was very little in the area in this regard. Well now I was sitting there in the disco with two girls, one five years younger and not necessarily pretty, and the other, a year older and quite "dressed up". Now I had no choice but to alternate between dancing with one and then with the other, and that for me, when I was such a talented dancer. During the course of the evening, it was already after midnight, on the 13th of November, when I was sitting at the table, I noticed that one knee kept bumping into mine and then it stayed. I think the next dances completed the approach of the older ones and it came as it had to come. It was wonderful. This then lasted a good 20 years.

Fall 1995

Since my competitor was becoming more and more aggressive with regard to the sale of newspapers and magazines, and he resorted to higher discounts for his colporteurs, I also had to react. Fortunately, I had a few Austrian publishers at the time that I could live on, because at least at that point there was nothing to be done with the said wholesalers. This was expressed in the fact that I could only sell my goods in secret, because every time I came to my customers - and they have been for years - there was always an Arab who could be assigned to the Robin company, with my buyer and thus prevented my sale. So, I had to get my magazines on sale in a roundabout way, because the buyer of my goods would have suffered financial disadvantages if they were seen to buy from me. But since the intellect of these supervisory bodies was not necessarily the highest, I kept bringing my goods up, even with difficulties. At that time, I was able to increase sales (about 600,000 Schilling balance sheet total) and the number of magazines enormously, so that my main supplier came to me in a large truck in the 20th district, where I had taken over my father's business premises. Often there were 2 pallets of goods with 10,000 magazines. At that time, I had climbed so far, probably due to competition reasons, that the week ran from Monday to Sunday. My partner Britta, since 1988, had rightly complained about that and I had to change that, and so I at least took the weekend off. But since I'm a little thick-headed and I'll do what I set out to do. So, it turned out the way it had to. In February 1998, I saw by chance that one of the two main suppliers had stopped delivering to the Robin company. A few days later I was able to officially establish that Robin's company was bankrupt. The bankruptcy sum was ATS 35 million. This amount certainly only included a small part of the deposits that Mr. Robin and his employees took from the colporteurs. It was rumored that he had stolen about 15 million schillings from his 100 to 200 colporteurs. I also learned that after the bankruptcy, this man only dared to go out on the street with bodyguards, probably because of the deposits withheld. Due to the bankruptcy, they were suddenly ready to give me the higher discount of 33.1 gross. Yes, but it was already too late by then.

July 1998 vacation

After I was never a fan of going on vacation, I still had a 2-week vacation on Crete, which to this day was probably the most beautiful of my life so far. There were also some experiences that stuck in my memory: We, my partner Britta and I, had borrowed a moped. The only stupid thing was that it was a semi-automatic. In other words, we were both sitting on this vehicle and I apparently let the clutch come too quickly and so my partner was sitting on the floor. Well, yes, halfway through the first obstacle. The landlord told us that we were only allowed to drive within 50 kilometers. We heard that and started our journey. But since this island has the disadvantage that, unlike us, you had to drive up and down every mountain, so we did that too and the 50 kilometers were forgotten. At the top of the mountain, we took a break and sat down on the grass. Then Britta suddenly said that she had seen something orange in the nearby grove. On the spur of the moment, we climbed under the fence and found an orange that was apparently overlooked during the harvest. Of course, we picked them right away. When we peeled it, an incredibly strong smell came into our noses and, above all, the enjoyment of this fruit was indescribable. Then we drove on, because we really wanted to go to the neighboring mountain to a monastery. Now it was noon and the sun was beating down pretty hard. The road wasn't paved, it was a gravel road. Nevertheless, we continued our journey. Suddenly I noticed that the moped was no longer reacting the way I wanted it to. We had a "flat". There was nothing far and wide. So, we had to push the vehicle in the utmost heat to the next gas station, which was safely 5 kilometers away. We hadn't told the landlord anything about what happened to us, but it was an experience for both of us. A few days later the hotel we were staying at was holding a jeep safari. As far as I can remember there were at least 10 jeeps packed with food and we drove across the island from north to south and east to west until we came to Elafonisi (the Maldives of Crete). Yes, we had enough food, from meat to salad, but what was missing was the cutlery. So, the women went to the sea, washed their hands and prepared the salads with their hands. In any case, it tasted good. A year later, again in July, we went on vacation to Lanzarote. We didn't like it too much there, as the whole area seemed very sterile to us, we couldn't go swimming in the sea either, the water was very cold (Atlantic Ocean). And again, a year later than July 2000 we stayed in a guesthouse in Styria for a few days, from where we went on some hikes. Since then, I have hardly had any vacations, except in 2017 to Italy in a few days by bus, which of course was more exhausting than taking the plane.

August 2000

When we came back from our Austrian vacation (3 days - Austria trip) in July 2000, Britta told me that she had abdominal pain and that she already had an appointment with the gynecologist about this. After this appointment, she called me immediately: I was of course worried and she said: What a good thing. What was that supposed to be? She said I'm going to be a dad. I was amazed, but we both took it for granted that we would be there for this child. The subject of abortion was never brought up, and it was good, at least by the time I found out about it. The due date was set at the beginning of March 2001.

On February 24, 2001, a Saturday, Britta woke me up in the morning and said that the time had come. For my job, I had a van that was getting on in years. It also snowed quite a bit the day before. So, we drove about 50 kilometers to the hospital without a heater in the car, because it didn't work. When they arrived at the hospital, they realized that it would take a while. So, we just went for a walk in the snow in the complex. In the evening I left her with the request that I be informed, regardless of the time of day, whether he was coming. No call came, so I drove to the hospital at 8 a.m. on Mardi Gras. When I opened the door to her room, she greeted me with the word: Surprise! A moment later the door opened again and a nurse brought my son to me. What I will remember forever was the moment when I held it in my hands for the first time. Indescribable.

My son at 10 months

1990 - 1991 apartment

Until then, I lived in the small apartment that I had when I was 18 years old. But since the property management and the owner of the apartment building wanted a general renovation of the house, I had to move one floor down to a slightly larger apartment. My apartment was merged with the neighboring apartment with the promise that I could move back into the 70 square meter apartment after the work was finished. This was also observed and in 1991 I moved into this apartment. But since my addiction grew worse over the years, which I was not aware of at the time, I fell behind with the rent payments. So, it came about, as it had to come, to an eviction suit. Britta and I were looking for an apartment. She found what she was looking for in an advertisement in a newspaper. A maisonette in the 2nd district with a rent of around 10,000 schillings. I pointed out that I could not afford it, but it was not necessarily accepted. Therefore, I returned the apartment in the 20th district without an eviction notice and moved to the 2nd district. But since my passion for gaming had not improved, but rather worsened, I was soon faced with the same result as in the 20th district. So, I looked for a Garcionerre myself in the 20th district that I might be able to afford.

1980 – addiction

It all started small, threw a few schillings into a machine and maybe won something once, but thrown that straight back into this bucket, because the big profit is coming. It took me around 15 years to realize that I was addicted to gambling. My partner Britta encouraged me to undergo therapy, but I also had to admit that I was addicted to this. So, I looked for help from Gamblers Anonymous. There were group therapies once a week and individual therapies by arrangement. The individual therapy caused a nervous breakdown in me because I had never experienced anything like it before, especially since the therapist had gone very deep. The group therapy was not necessarily successful because I got into the car after the session and ended up in an arcade again. So, I saw no point in this therapy. Apparently, I had to do more in this regard. Britta asked me about progress with this therapy, or whether I had stopped playing. I answer this with "yes", that I would have stopped playing. As far as I know, that was the only time in 20 years of partnership where I had lied to her. But I also had the habit of skillfully avoiding sensitive questions, especially those of a financial nature. So, at that time I saw no way out and the thoughts of suicide came closer and closer.

June 2001 bankruptcy

On February 15, 2001, ten days before the birth of my son, I had a bankruptcy negotiation. This was preceded by submitting my own initiative or my commercial understanding. I spoke to the judge about this and we were able to achieve a compensation rate of around 13.84% that we could offer the creditors. At this hearing in the Commercial Court of Vienna, two creditor representatives from around 20 creditors were present. The offered quota was not accepted by both lawyers of the credit protection association and AKV. In mid-June 2001, the municipal authorities in the 20th district asked me to return the two trade licenses that I had for almost 9 years. The reason for this was that I had accumulated quite a bit of debt over time. I did this and was then registered as unemployed. My father, who was retired at the time, bought his trade license for the magazine wholesaling again. And so, business went on, but that didn't stop me from playing and, above all, from doing something about it.

2000 magistrate / finance

Around the turn of the millennium, my customers kept coming to me and asking for confirmation of their income. In other words, the respective offices require a corresponding proof of income when extending or re-submitting a residence permit. It was officially expected that a person living in Austria should have a minimum income of € 700. For me it was easy to determine because there was a fixed discount and retail price. So, I wrote them to you if the amount was sufficient and you received your corresponding paper from the magistrate. On no day had I received money for issuing this paper, at least not until 2006. For me, these people were also independent merchants and also had to transfer the amount I had written to the assessment channel. Whether they actually practiced that is beyond my knowledge. But I also defined this on the papers on display.

March 2006 death of my father

In February 25, 2006 my parents came to us, Britta, my son Gregor and me to Lower Austria. My partner invited her for my son's 5th birthday. After retiring in 1992, my father gained about ten pounds. He wasn't fat, but enjoyed the meal to the full. Of course, my son had already found this out when he was 5 years old, so he bombarded my father with pastries at the snack. Grandpa take the cake, I know you like to nibble too. A quarter of an hour later he came with a donut and Grandpa took it and ate. The next morning in the shop at around 7 o'clock my father was already there, as usual. We got in the car and drove to a customer. On the drive, he told me that he had slept so badly that night. In addition, he got up every half hour to go to the toilet with corresponding chest pain. When we were back in business an hour later, I urgently asked him to go to our family doctor in the same street to have a look. Well, yes, it was winter on February 26th, 2006 and my father went to the doctor with great reluctance only in his sweater. After an hour my phone rang and it was his turn. I should bring him a jacket to the internist down the street, because the family doctor would have sent him to the internist immediately with the suspicion of a heart attack. This doctor did not allow herself to be taken there for a diagnosis and immediately called the ambulance to take them to a hospital. Arriving at the hospital, the suspicion that the two doctors suspected was confirmed. There he was checked through for 11 days and released on March 10, a Friday. On March 13th in the morning, as always, I came into the shop around 7 a.m. and my father was already there. Since the first thing I make in the morning was put down a coffee, I did that that day too. Meanwhile, I noticed that my father was going into the hallway toilet. As usual, I set up a coffee for my mother on the first floor of the same house and went to the back of the store in the stairwell. I noticed that the light was on in our corridor toilet (opaque glass) and I knew it could only be my father, but 10 to 15 minutes had passed when I last saw him. I then went to my parents' apartment and talked to her for a while. When I passed the toilet again, the light was still on and went into the store, but no one was there. So, I went to the toilet again and knocked on the window, but there was no reaction. In the meantime, the neighbor who lived next door had come out of her apartment. But since there was no reaction in the toilet, I had no choice but to smash the door window with my elbow. Thereupon saw him already sitting leaning against the wall and with blood from his nose. The neighbor immediately called the ambulance and also brought me clothes for the hallway floor so I could put it on. The rescue was there pretty quickly and they tried to bring him back with a defibrillator, but in vain. The ambulance informed the medical officer that he should determine the death. In the meantime, the police also came, where a man stood by the dead man until the medical officer came. This came after about 3 hours. The first of his questions was whether there were any recent findings that I could of course answer. When he had looked through it, he said: With the cocktail this was nothing surprising and dying in Vienna on Monday was unfavorable, because we have a traffic jam. If I had not been in mourning, I would not have been able to control myself over such statements. But what still touched me was that I had to tell my mother, who was in her apartment. And the next problem was to inform my brother, who had been out of contact for about 20 years, that our father had died. He had fallen out with his parents over the inheritance he was entitled to. But he was there within an hour without any bad words. On March 24, 2006, we had him buried in the Vienna Central Cemetery. Then when the coffin was lowered, I had a decisive event. I inherited a lot from my father, including the fact that we can't talk about problems and that we kept avoiding them, now it was too late.

March 2006 extortion

On March 14th, I returned my father's two trade licenses to the responsible magistrate in the 20th district. I already knew the handling in this regard. On March 20, my phone rang and the number was withheld. At the other end was a man who didn't tell me a name, even though I asked several times in the course of the conversation. He said I should continue to write the confirmations that I have been writing since the turn of the millennium. When I asked why I should do that, he told me about the circumstances of the place where my son grew up that you could only know if you were there. E.g., when he went to kindergarten today and the like. That of course pissed me off and I threatened him. His answer was only that after the previous call he would send me a foreigner and I would have to issue a confirmation. I would have to charge € 10 for one month and € 15 for several months, which these people would then pay. In the beginning I refused, of course, arguing that I could no longer write that because I was not entitled to the trade, but over time the information about my son, what he was doing, became more and more real and I had to assume that he stayed near Gregor, which was proven a year later. In the village with around 800 inhabitants and an area of 34 square kilometers, strangers naturally attract attention, especially when they are driving in front of public buildings, such as a school or kindergarten. Now I had the choice of going to the police and filing a report, if accepted, and protection for my son will be assigned for a week or two, and then I have to tremble whether the man can think of anything. The other option was for me to do it my way, which I read myself to do regardless of the consequences. So, the calls came several times a week with suppressed numbers and the foreigners, whom I only knew partially, received their confirmations against payment. When I asked the people where they had contact from, I got no information. So, I decided to follow these people, but at least at the beginning this was hopeless. In the meantime, it was already autumn 2007, my son went to elementary school. In the village, a man was observed in various places where it was assumed that he was a pedophile, as he was seen repeatedly at school or kindergarten. But this was a mistake, the whole thing was meant for me. One Friday after school, like every school day, my son took the school bus home. Since the way about 500 meters from the exit point to the place of residence was not entirely visible, a car suddenly came from the side street, stopped at my son's and the passenger door opened. A man spoke to him and wanted to give him candy. My son reacted once and immediately ran towards the house where my partner had been waiting for him. She saw the vehicle and also called the police, only until they came the driver was over the mountains despite the dead end. When my son told me about this on the same day, Friday evening, I spoke to my partner about it and told her that this was not a pedophile, it would have applied to me, but she stuck to the pedophile's version.

December 13, 2006

It was a Friday and again a 13th. I was sitting in the shop that had two exits, one to the courtyard of the house and one to the street. I wrote on my programs, as I had for a long time, and was absorbed accordingly. Suddenly there was a knock on the courtyard door; I had locked the other door. It was around noon and assumed it was a house party. When I opened the door, there was a man about 190 cm tall with a well-groomed appearance. He identified himself with his name and ID as the "Official Director" of the Vienna Tax Office. Now he said, holding an A4 piece of paper in his hand, that he was holding a confirmation in his hand where my company stamp and my signature could be found on it. He also claimed that it was printed on both sides. He also asked if he could come in, which I didn't refuse. But then I immediately had to refute his claims. On the one hand, I had never given papers out of my hand that were printed on both sides, and on the other hand, I hadn't put a stamp on such letters either, that was already included in the program that I had written for them myself. I never had the letter on which this claim was based. Now he said whether he could look into my stand PC, which I did not refuse. He also wanted to look at and take photos of my bank statements, which I had on the shelf behind me, which I did not refuse, because I was not aware of any guilt. Now he began to take his minutes. When he asked how such confirmations of income came about, from when and why, he concluded the visit with the question of what I would have received for it, and he meant not only money, but also natural goods. What should I answer him now, because in the meantime I realized that he needed his sense of achievement, and on the other hand I still had my blackmailer at this point, who put me under quite a bit of pressure? So, I answered his question with the answer: I have not received anything in return. His reaction was that he didn't believe this. In the following year he came to my shop twice more without prior notice and kept looking. Last time, he asked if he could take the stand PC with him to the tax office, which

I answered in the affirmative after some time to think about it. Time to think about the fact that it wouldn't necessarily have been beneficial to the computer, but of course I had nothing to hide. I had it back in working order within two days, but he didn't tell me whether something illegal was found or not. So far so good or not. In autumn 2007 there was then an "invitation" to the tax office in the 22nd district. There he offered me the results of his tax audit, as it is called in financial German. He had already indicated to me that he would have to appreciate me if I didn't tell him what I would do for the issuance of income statements and so we agreed on this name. His estimate was that he thought I would have received € 100 for each confirmation, starting with 1998 and ending in 2008. In other words, an income of € 40,000 and an "accommodating" expense minus 50 %. So, in his eyes, I had earned € 20,000 year after year with this work, which was also reflected in the corresponding income tax modest. In one fell swoop, I had two claims from the tax office and health insurance company in the amount of a 6-digit amount, against which I immediately responded by appealing to the then finance senate as the higher level of the tax offices, today, as far as I know, it is the financial procurator. All appointments, and that was 9 years at that time, were rejected or rejected by the individual offices. The state or its officials are mostly right, the citizen hardly. What I had not expected at the time, however, was the fact that this official director, not only viewed it as a financial offense, but also as a violation of the law. After completing his examination in 2008, he passed on the data he had constructed, for which he could never provide evidence, to the Vienna Public Prosecutor for the purpose of checking for illegality. In addition to my appointments in 2008, for the years 2006 to 2008, when I finally got hold of my blackmailer, I prepared income tax returns for these 3 years for a total of € 2,500 in income from the preparation of income statements, which have not been taken into account to this day. In the years 1998 up to and including 2005 I had no intake due to this circumstance. This public prosecutor's office also reacted in the form of the respective district courts, where between 2009 and 2011 I was "asked" to appear as a witness to around 100 subpoenas. The process there was always the same. The basic tenor of my interrogations by the respective court was always the same. I was asked whether I had issued this paper and of course why. There was always a foreigner sitting across from me who, among other things, was accused by Municipal Department 35 of having obtained or bought a residence permit with such a confirmation. The paper on which this process was based was presented to me and I had to determine whether I had issued it or not. 90% of them were my papers, but there were also forgeries, which is what the chief executive officer claims. The accused foreigners, whom I knew at least by appearance, got, if they were really found guilty, 2 months to three years, conditionally, no more. As I already mentioned, in May 2008 I finally got hold of the blackmailer by following a supposed colporteur once again after he received a confirmation from me. With "powerful" arguments I implored this man to delete my number immediately and never to call me again. I didn't have much hope, but he kept to it for whatever reason and I never saw or heard from him again, but had also changed my cell phone number. I had never been able to find out what he got out of it or not. In the spring of 2010, I suddenly received a registered letter from the Vienna Public Prosecutor - Vienna Criminal Court. In it I was asked to appear as a suspect at the public prosecutor's office for questioning. I followed that up and sat across from the public prosecutor. I was accused of issuing income statements that did not comply with the law. Since this middle-aged man had a few files in front of him, he leafed through them and asked me whether he knew the name he was reading there and, above all, how such papers came about. I then confirmed his questions, but asked him to show me the confirmations, where I could again recognize about 10% fakes, which he also saw. As far as I can remember, he was with him a second time this year. The whole thing was only questioning of an accused on the part of the public prosecutor. In the spring of 2011, I received another registered letter, but this time from the Vienna Criminal Court, where I was supposed to go as the defendant. I met a judge there, the public prosecutor, whom I knew by now, and my public defender who, at my first meeting with him, had complained that he had to read through 6000 pages of court documents for the trial. Now it came to this negotiation, where naturally all sides asked questions. The question of whether I had received money for this issue of the papers was of secondary importance, just as it was during the interrogation by the public prosecutor. I was able to convince the judge as best as possible with my answers and arguments. My attorney was more reluctant, just digging a precedent that had very little to do with my indictment. The prosecutor was a little more persistent and asked rather brisk questions. Result of this trial, the judge announced the verdict, 24 months' imprisonment, means no prison. After the verdict was pronounced, he instructed me on my decision about it; To accept the judgment immediately, 3 days to consider or appeal immediately. I really didn't expect that, because I assumed that I could leave the court as a free man and innocent. So, I looked at my defense attorney and showed him 3 fingers for 3 days to think about it. But seeing that the prosecutor saw my hesitation, he said that he would appeal or take legal action. In February 2012 the second hearing before the Higher Regional Court of Vienna took place, where I assumed that the verdict would be in my favor. So, I entered the courtroom at the prescribed time and found a judges' senate. When my data was checked, one of the judges spoke to me: The judgment of the Vienna Criminal Court will be changed to 16 months conditional and 8 months unconditional. My reaction to that: It can't be that! The judge said: If you did not understand the verdict, you will have to be detained for 8 months. For me, a world collapsed. On the one hand, I had issued these papers in good faith until I was blackmailed; on the other hand, I wanted to protect my son, which went badly in the pants. I almost never had a financial advantage and was punished for it. Of course, I asked my lawyer what else could be done in this regard, but had to realize that there was no appeal to this judgment, only a petition. But he immediately gave me no hope that something in this decision of the Higher Regional Court would change as a result of such a petition. But I asked him to do it. But it was also unsuccessful. So, I then received a letter from the court, where I had to be at the Simmering prison by April 10, 2012 at the latest, to begin my 8-month prison sentence.

2006 to 2011 all about care

When my father died in March 2006, as already mentioned, I was once again facing an eviction from my Garcionerre in the 20th district. Now, after the death of her husband, my mother was completely on her own, and after almost 53 years of marriage, the roof over my head was removed, so what was left but to move into a 75 square meter apartment with the argument on my part to give her mutual supervision, because she was quite depressed after death. At the time, I couldn't say whether my decision was right or not, and she had already had 2 strokes behind her. At the time her husband passed away, she weighed around 80 kilos, was not fat but stocky. The first year with her in an apartment was pretty good, we went shopping, to the doctor and for examinations. At this point she had to take about 10 tablets a day due to her previous illnesses. Among them was a psychotropic drug, where I had to go to a neurologist rather than a family doctor every time to get the prescription. I think it was prescribed because she had become increasingly depressed. It would also be said that I did my work in the same house, only separated by a courtyard. Means I was on the ground floor and she was in the apartment on the first floor. In the second year, her condition began to deteriorate rapidly, she ate less and less and did not want to go outside. I can remember one episode where the two of us were shopping at the grocery store about 300 meters and she couldn't go any further after she paid for the purchase. So, I sat her down in the shop, ran the 300 meters back to the shop and fetched my toboggan, which I had had for years, drove it into the shop, put it on the toboggan with great reluctance and drove it home. I didn't care what it looked like. You not necessarily. The whole thing looked like I spent in the apartment with her from Monday to Friday and went to see my family in Lower Austria on Friday evening, Gregor and Britta. But since she shouldn't necessarily be alone at the weekend, my brother came by for two to three hours on Saturday and that turned into a farce almost every time. Once he called me because he couldn't find the medication, another time because of some triviality. That is to say, he was not a great help to me in this regard either. But since the growing depression, paranoia and dementia were added, caring for her person became more and more difficult, that is to say, the 24-hour care was fully used. During the day, since she no longer had a concept of time, she slept and during the night when I wanted to sleep in the next room, she haunted the apartment. Didn't even have to pick her up in the living room at midnight or later and put her back to bed. In addition, she no longer had an overview of what household items she had. It happened that at 11 o'clock in the morning she stood on the balcony and called my name loudly because she was standing, Peter, needed at least two tubes of toothpaste. Then I came in the courtyard, saw her gesticulating wildly on the balcony and said she should look in the box, as far as I know there were at least 10 tubes of toothpaste there. All she said was that she would know what she needed and not me. So, I had to buy her the 11 and 12 tubes immediately and immediately. I never did that, that I went shopping. The only time I had to breathe was the times when she came from one hospital to the next, where I only had to visit her for about an hour, because there was nothing more in there. It became more and more difficult for me to speak to her because she saw no perspective. In the individual hospitals, I think she "visited" almost all of the hospitals in Vienna, but they kept them for a maximum of 10 days, because physically they could not find anything and as far as the psyche was concerned, no one could help her. Now my dear brother, with whom, as I said, I had no contact for about 20 years, came to the glorious idea of incapacitating his mother. To do this, he went to the responsible district court and filed the application. My opinion on this was that she was certainly still sane, even if she was already well on the way to becoming insane. So, one evening, after prior notification, a lawyer from the district court came to our apartment. My mother and we two sons were present. At the beginning he put his questions to my mother, who answered them correctly, but then my brother, who had made the application, received a rather solid instruction from this lawyer. He said that the woman was fully sane and why he had made the application, which of course he could not answer. This request was therefore rejected. Up until this point, my relationship with my brother was still reasonably well-mannered and factual. After that it got worse and worse, up to and including physical attacks on his part in the presence of our mother. In September 2010, she walked around the apartment again during the day and fell in the living room. I was just out and about at the time. At that time, she had a home help three times a day for about 4 years, because I wasn't always there and the result was a key safe at the entrance to the apartment, because of course the home help and rescue services were also used. In addition, she had a wristband with an emergency button that she could use if necessary. So that day the rescue came, who also informed me that something had happened to my mother, and they also came in using the key safe.

They then took her to the hospital, where it was found that she had a rib drilled into her lungs when she fell in the apartment. Now drove to the nearest hospital again and talked to the head doctor of the department. She asked me if my mother would be cared for 24 hours a day after she was released. But I had to answer this question with no, because I was physically and mentally exhausted not only because of it, but also because of my addiction. It would have to be sent in advance that immediately after my father's death in March 2006, my brother had applied for a place in an old people's home for her. It would have been easier for him then to see her in a home a month later. When, after about 2 years, I received a promise for the home in the 20th district, I knew this house inside and out, and she tortured me with the decision of what to do: to the home or not. In this regard, it should be noted that this home was in one of their familiar surroundings and, since it has not been in place for long, is also very beautiful. My argument was that it would be her own decision and that I would neither advise nor advise against it. My brother, of course, immediately persuaded her to take the place. After a few weeks and months, she refused. Now, as I said, she was in the hospital and the municipality of Vienna was looking for a place in a nursing home, which she got at the end of 2010 in a newly opened home in the 22nd district. There on the 8th floor with an elevator, she was given a room with about 20 square meters. As far as I could tell, she was one of the youngest at the time, aged 78. There was a common room next to the rooms where the inmates came together to gossip or play games. I remember saying several times that she should go out of her room and talk to the others. But her paranoia or dementia was so far advanced that she no longer wanted to be around people, because they could do something to her, as I had to hear from her in various hospitals when she saw people with white coats and who wanted to do something to her. She did not allow my argument that these were only medical staff who wanted to help her. On March 2, 2011, I went to her home almost every day to visit her. On that day she was hardly available, nor was I able to talk to her. When I drove home, I had my premonitions. During the night, as usual, I turned off my cell phone. In the morning when I turned it on again, I saw a text message from the home. My premonition was confirmed, she fell asleep peacefully in the arms of a nurse that night. Now we buried our mother in the same grave where my father was. I was now alone in a 75 square meter apartment with my belongings and a rent of just under € 500.

May 2011 Neocathomenat

My relationship with my mother wasn't exactly what I had at the time, but she was there for me even in my childhood, if only to a limited extent. So, I was in a bit of a dilemma as far as she was concerned. On a beautiful spring day in early May, I was walking along the Danube Canal in my old clothes one Sunday, then sat on a bench and started typing on my cell phone. Since I already had very limited eyesight at this point due to growing cataracts, I did not see too much. Suddenly the sun that was shining on my face darkened. When I looked up, there were two people in front of me whom I could barely make out. One woman asked me if I believed in God after introducing herself as Anna. She also introduced the second lady, but I don't remember her name. It would have to be sent in advance that I would have avoided such a discussion at any time. This question, which I don't want to answer here, resulted in a half-hourly conversation and at the end said to me: I'll invite you next Saturday evening at 8 p.m. I'll write down Wolfgang's phone number for you, should something come up in the meantime. What was that? Two women who were a good 10 years older than me invite me. They also told me that they were from the Neo-Catholic, part of the Catholic Church and not a sect. Okay, now I had a phone number from a certain Wolfgang and an invitation. What is that supposed to be? Now I lay in bed every evening and pondered this invitation.

So, this Saturday came and I thought I had money like none and of course I was curious what that was. So, as usual, I left home earlier and got there in the 20th district at 7:30 p.m. As I entered the hall where the whole thing was to take place, I saw a man at the other end of the room who was setting up folding chairs. When he saw me at the door, he came up to me, held out his hand and said he was Wolfgang. Only then did I realize that this must be a priest, because he was dressed in black from top to bottom. When he then asked my name, I was a bit perplexed and I started to stutter and said: My name is Eduard. This name stayed with me for a while, until I could persuade him to call me Edi. He also asked if I could help him set up the armchairs, which of course I did willingly. Now it was almost 8 p.m. and I expected that some older people would show up, the 20 or so armchairs were ready and so I sat down on one of them. Then the second door of the room opened and a girl about 16 years old came in with a guitar on her back. Over time the room filled up and I discovered that I was one of the oldest. When the whole thing started shortly after 8 p.m., of course, I had to introduce myself, which I had never liked to do before. It then turned out that it was a Eucharist with two readings and a gospel from the Bible. I still had in the back of my mind that my grandmother, who was Catholic, had often moved me to mass in the Catholic Church during my school days and I already thought back then that it was nothing for me, all the old people, praying and kneeling and pray again. But it was a little different and not just the participants. The two readings from the Bible were prepared and read by the individual participants themselves. Wolfgang, who portrayed himself as a priest, only presided and had to read the Gospel and then analyze all the readings in a sermon. We, all participants, could also announce what the respective reading would have told us and that voluntarily. I also liked that the guitar wasn't just there to look at, but that a song was always intoned between the individual readings, and we all sang along with it. Well, this was completed around 10 p.m. and I was informed that there would be a liturgy of words on the following Tuesday at 8 p.m. After I had promised me this kind of a fair, I went back on Tuesday. I then became a brother of what was then the 10th community in the Neokathomenat, which I also practiced for seven years and which personally brought me a lot. The process in this community was always the same, 3 to 4 people from this group had to prepare the respective liturgy or the Eucharist at one of the 3 to 4 people at home a few days beforehand and then present it on that day. It was not always easy to find enough people to take part. We also had a community Sunday every one or two months and about twice a year a community weekend in a hotel in Lower Austria. When I came to this community in May 2011, it had only existed for half a year. In other words, you didn't know each other very well, but this changed over the years, as you kept preparing with someone else and thus saw the environment in which he or she was moving. At that time, I became friends with two sisters, Maria and Giada. Maria was born in Poland and studied in Austria, Giada was a young exchange student from Capri / Italy, around 20 years old. I had done a lot with both of them, but Giada had to go back to Italy in the summer of 2012 when she already spoke perfect German. What connected me with Maria was that she indulged my addiction as much as I did, just not as excessively.

April 2012 prison sentence

So, on April 10th I drove with my belongings to the 11th district to begin my prison sentence, as they were getting fewer and fewer. This was preceded by the fact that two months earlier I had another eviction suit with the execution date, May 10, 2012 on my neck. So, I had little time to vacate the apartment in the 20th district. Maria and my colleague, to whom I will come later, were of great help to me because I was in custody at that time. When I got to the detention center, I was searched thoroughly and then put in the closed ward in a cell about 10 square meters in pairs. At the beginning I was instructed what I should and shouldn't do, as well as being informed which department there was. There was only an hour's walk in the courtyard during the day, weather permitting. The first two months, of course, I had enough time, talking to my fellow inmate wasn't always easy, so I took the Bible and read it from beginning to end, despite the cataracts. After two months, I was transferred to the relaxed prison system, where one could work in the detention center. There were 6 to 10 people in the room who had worked in various departments. But since I am a person who enjoys his freedom, I let myself be transferred again and ended up in the open air. That means getting up at 4:30 a.m. and driving from the 11th district to the barracks in the 14th district, where I was assigned to gardening with other prisoners. Since it was not exactly pleasant to stand in the sun all day in July August 2012, we longed for the end of work at 4 p.m. After that we had to be back in the detention center by 6 p.m. sharp. The fellowship I joined a year earlier gave me tremendous support during that time. This was expressed in the fact that for each and every day of my visit, three of my current siblings came to visit me and gave me consolation. Since I also had the opportunity to spend the weekend outside of the institution with the outdoor department, I was able to attend a community Sunday, among other things. What also had to be noted here was that all of my relatives, including some in the form of 4 cousins and an aunt and uncle, didn't show up during visiting hours, I don't even want to talk about my brother, because he knew that I am sitting. In addition, my sister Maria put a lot of pressure on me to reconcile with my parents, because I made her guilty for where I was now. So, it happened on a Sunday morning when I was allowed to go out for this conversation at 8 o'clock. Well, yes, they were both dead, what should I talk about with stones. But since the cemetery was near the detention center, I got off the tram and went to the grave. At first, I didn't know what to say, but then I think I talked to them for about half an hour and I ended up with tears running down my cheeks. When I went back to the tram, I felt 10 pounds lighter. Since then, I have made peace with my parents, even if they were only stones and an evil word about my parents will come from my lips again, I am not entitled to, I should do better, but it seems I didn't succeed either, at least until now. One morning when I was driving back to the barracks to work, an accident happened to me. We had the option of catering in the barracks. That means we were able to have breakfast, lunch and now and then food in the form of cans for the evening. Well, I went, as usual, to have breakfast at 6:30 a.m. and eat a hearty fresh roll. Suddenly I noticed that my upper dentition was broken in the middle.

Thus, in the evening in detention, I arranged for a visit to the dentist to be allowed, because my bite was not given. I got it too and had to stay in the institution that day. It is to be sent in advance that I did not have health insurance during my detention and that the costs of any treatment were covered by the judiciary's budget. So, I came to a dentist who wasn't necessarily the best, but who had charged the judiciary a lot for mending my teeth. In the time, I had already registered it, my cataract worsened so much that in the end I only had 2% eyesight. That means I had to catch the curb with the help of my feet. Was wrongly assuming that this operation could also be done while in custody, but two days after release from custody on December 12th I had the right eye for the operation and a week later the other.

Dismissed December 10, 2012

On that day I was released and was now standing on the street with about € 700, - a vision of 2% and my measly belongings and without a roof over my head. But since a brother named Werner had offered to move into his cabinet in the 8th district while I was in custody, I gladly accepted. He only said until I found something. Since I now had too much money in my pocket, it naturally itched, I did not have such an appearance during detention, although it would probably have been based on the time. So, it happened as it had to, I continued playing and after a while Brother Werner asked me how far my apartment search had progressed. After seeing that I hadn't put too much zeal into it, he rightly gave me an ultimatum. I let that pass too, and so I had to apply to the municipality of Vienna for a homeless asylum, which I also got in the 16th district together with a second in a room of 20 square meters. According to my imagination, I had imagined that you wouldn't have to pay anything for it, but that was a mistake. Certainly not the amount for a rent, but at least it was € 160 that I was able to pay at the beginning. But in the course of time that was no longer possible. In spite of social counselors, they were forced to remove me from the house. What now? My employer and friend Kamal offered to accommodate me in the basement of his business, without toilet and water, since the year was already advanced and winter was just around the corner, I had to accept that, of course without the knowledge of the other house parties. I wasn't alone down there, I also had pets in the form of mice that would run over my face at times when I was sleeping. That was probably the time when I thought at least once a week what I was living for. I hadn't achieved anything, on the contrary, I ruined everything, at the age of 11 I had to lie to my son that I had to work in Berlin and therefore only called him once a week from the prison. My suicidal thoughts were already very extreme back then. Of course, my brothers and sisters in the community also knew about the whole misery, but they couldn't help me either, even if that went as far as the catechist.

December 24, 2014 ends

Now it was Christmas, one like it had been in previous years. I slept in the basement, had pets with me and € 20 in my wallet. There were still a few groceries, because over time I was able to live on € 6 a day for food and smoking. Well, what do you do with this money, you go to the nearest gambling hall and the amount was gone? At this point in time, it was decided in the municipality of Vienna that the small game of chance would be discontinued on January 1st, 2015. Means that all the machines that I fed for over 30 years were shut down, but only in Vienna and not in Lower Austria. Well, the new year came, there were no more machines in Vienna and money was back in my pocket. Now I had the opportunity to get on the train, drive to a suburb of Vienna and continue to eat these buckets. But that was not the case, why I still cannot explain myself to this day, but no matter I will certainly not question it. In other words, after a good 30 years and the resulting difficulties, I was cured of this addiction on December 24, 2014. From that day on I had never touched a machine again. Of course, I couldn't answer what I had gambled away over time, but I assume that it was definitely a 7-digit amount. In other words, I had paid my taxes through profit and sales tax with my work and that not too scarce, at least from my side, but I cannot judge whether this ended up with the respective offices such as the tax office and municipality. What was interesting was that when I had my forced residency in 2012, I didn't have to play and hardly in freedom, it went on again. How did it go on now? In February 2015 I looked for a place in the homeless shelter again and got it immediately in the 16th district. Now everything happened in rapid succession. The social worker who looked after me put a lot of pressure on me to be assigned a community apartment. The fee for the place in the € 160, - were no longer a problem, so they were paid regularly. Since I already made an appearance in January 2013 about a community apartment, I didn't really hope that it would work this time. In 2013 they asked me to confirm my registration and lease contracts for the past three years. I was able to fulfill the registration confirmation, but of course I couldn't provide a rental agreement. The argument that I was an Austrian citizen and was born in Vienna didn't help either. I was so furious at the time that I let myself be carried away by saying that this negative notice should be issued to me, because I need this paper for a specific location. Well back again. The social worker in this home asked me to deposit a certain amount there in the house month after month so that I would have money for the apartment when I left the home. On July 1, 2015, I received a small apartment with 36 square meters in the 20th district, where I still live today. But since I had almost no furniture, I had to buy everything from built-in kitchens to cabinets. Since the apartment is on the 5th floor, a roommate from the homeless shelter helped me. What was going on, the gambling addiction was gone, I had my own apartment, where there are no rent arrears to this day and above all I suddenly had more than 10 euros in my wallet. That was a wonderful feeling and nothing has changed so far. In other words, I brought myself to life, what it was when I was a player, I wouldn't necessarily assign it to that.

February 2016 normal life

At the beginning of 2016, a postcard fluttered into my mailbox. I read this and found that it was an online portal where you could register for free. After it was free, I did that too. The whole thing was a website with a good hundred different groups, depending on their interests. Since I've always been a curious person, I looked at the groups and found about 4 to 5 groups that spoke to me. For two of these, I set activities at 50+ clubs and 60+ clubs, which also corresponded to the age of the members. Now Helmut, the admin of the group 60+ Treff, organized restaurant visits every two weeks at 6 p.m. in the evening. Each time in a different restaurant. Since I didn't know anything like that from my past, it was a pleasure for me to always eat well there and to gossip for about 3 to 4 hours with the 8 to 10 people who were there. The other group, 50+, was a challenge for me from the start. Then the admin wrote, I forgot my name, again every 2 weeks on Friday evening at 6 p.m. a meeting in a market stall in the 3rd district. In this group, however, the focus was not on food, but much more on society. However, since these meetings were not optimally organized, only a handful came to these gatherings, but not much more was possible, there was not enough space for more at this stand. The admin Helmut from the group 60+ Treff did this much more precisely until his death in 2019. I always took my friend Roman with me to both meetings because he was single at the time, but I will come back to him later. As I said, there wasn't too much going on in the 50+ group and so I took the initiative to put meetings online every 2 weeks through this group. The group had around 100 members at that time and so I advertised a meeting in an eatery and not in a market stall buffet in the portal. At the beginning there were maybe 7 to 8 people from this group and of course the main focus was not on food, but on conversation and conversations. It was interesting that with each and every one of them there were consistently more women than men were present every 2 weeks. That means at times it happened that Roman and I were the only men. But after I loved to surround myself with women, which was also a new experience for me, I received the women accordingly. That means kissing left and right, where I then realized that this had an impact on the subsequent quality of the conversation. It was a bit cumbersome at the beginning, but over time more and more came to these meetings. The number of members in this group also rose steadily, until the end with a good 500 members. Since I was not the admin of this group, of course there was hostility to other members of this group, among other things with the argument that this was a partner exchange, which I put back on the website with corresponding comments. In 2018 and 2019 I had the idea that you don't necessarily have to go to a pub, but that there is also culture and light sports. These meetings were not necessarily accepted by the members. It was cabaret, bowling, billiards or mini golf, so no fancy things. Only about 5 to 6 people came to such meetings, so I returned to the local meetings. When the pandemic came in 2020, we had our last meeting in the 3rd district in February. A few months later I was informed by Pamela that she could no longer find the group 50+ Treff on the website. But since such meetings could not take place with lockdown and other restrictions, I did not notice this fact. I investigated it and found that both the group 60+ Treff, which however had no activities after the death of the admin, and the group 50+ Treff and its members had been removed from this page. The background was, and it became apparent some time beforehand, that the software (allegedly Ubuntu) behind it had crashed and new software was installed via this website. Since I now call myself a programmer, I wrote to this company, the owners of this site, about twice to find out what would have happened there. The answer was that some old groups could no longer be restored. Of course, I also commented that this could very well be done, but also with an enormous expenditure of time, because the data must be available, you just have to read it out and add it to the new portal.

Fall 2015 dance events

My friend Roman, whom I had known for a number of years, once asked me whether we could go dancing at the Pensioners' Association in Vienna on a Saturday, which we did then. And so, we went dancing every Saturday evening either in the 2nd district or in the 20th district until the pandemic came in 2020 and of course there were no more events. I wasn't a pensioner at the time, but what the heck, I liked it, even if I'm not a professional dancer (hopeless case).

Family

Well, yes, I probably had that for about 10 to 11 years, but when I went to boarding school, the relationship must have deteriorated, because there, whether I wanted to or not, 90% of my decisions had to be made alone.

In doing so, hardly anyone was at my side with advice. Whether I would have accepted it or not is also questionable. In my childhood, I had a good relationship with my 3 cousins on weekends, who are a little younger than me, with the fourth I only had contact twice, at their own request. That means, I saw the 3 girls in the 11th district almost every weekend. As for my brother, we were one heart and one soul for about 16 years. That changed when he said he had to have a wife now. When he was around 30 to 35 years old, he demanded his inheritance in cash from his parents in my presence in Lower Austria. The background was that he was now married and had two daughters and said he had to build an existence here and now in Germany. Since this request was expressed with physical strength, he "said goodbye" for a good 20 years. We had no contact with him until shortly before our father's death. Even today I don't have any contact with him and I don't know about him or me about where we live. As for my son, who is now 20 years old, it should be said that in 2012 I couldn't tell him that I was in custody, but that I had to work abroad, he was 11 years old at the time. My partner and I had agreed on this. I had a good relationship with him at least until I was forced to stay in the 11th district, even if it was only on the weekend. However, since in my opinion he was informed by a dear relative of my ex-partner where I really was in 2012, despite several attempts since April 2018, I have not had any contact, the last time I saw him was on July 15, 2017. The relationship with my mother was actually only a good one in my first years of life, but since we were very different characters, that changed at the latest with the boarding school, but that didn't change the fact that I stood by her in the last years of her life. But what struck me a lot and that still concerns me today, that I could never talk to my father and he probably couldn't talk to me either.

Friends

Over the years I have certainly had several friends whom I am trying to classify here, although I am not really entitled to it, but as I said, that's how I see it. Among my best friends were certainly those from Lower Austria, whom I already knew when I was 12 years old learned. However, since they were spread across the entire federal state of

Lower Austria, the friendship ended after around 15 to 20 years. As for my Viennese friend, I still don't know why he never prevented me from becoming addicted to gambling. But I would like to credit him that he would not have been able to do so. In 2005 or 2006 I had problems with my stand PC in the shop and, as money was usually tight, I looked for a computer repair, which I also found in the 20th district. There I came to a cellar restaurant two streets away. When I saw the person named Kamal, I realized that it had to be an Arab and addressed him that way, since I had dealt with these people for years before. He replied to my Arabic words and also said that he was born in Alexandria but is now an Austrian citizen. A year or two later he moved two streets down to a restaurant on the ground floor, where he employed me some time later, he is responsible for hardware and I for software. He was the one who offered me shelter in the basement the year I didn't have any. About a year later, a slightly older gentleman came to our shop in the 20th district, as it turned out, he was 20 years older than me. He said he had problems with his own website, since the software was adapted, he no longer knew his way around and he wanted to add a few things. I might like to see what I did on the spot. There I found a fairly large website that he had worked on himself for years, and I read my way into that system. In the end, I was finally able to fix the conversation problems he was having with the new system. A friendship developed from both encounters, which continues to this day and which I wouldn't want to miss either. Yes, connections were made from the groups 60+ clubs and 50+ clubs, but they fizzled out again with the pandemic.

Partnerships

The first partnership with my colleague at the research center disappointed me a little, as I was a little snubbed that she had forced me and a child to move under the same roof as her parents, whereby her father accepted me very well, but his wife did who had to know everything annoyed me a bit. As for my second wife in my life, she was undisputedly the woman of my life, otherwise the partnership would not have lasted over 20 years. That it broke up, despite the 8-year-old son at the time, is probably 95% my fault. I had only found in retrospect that we never talked about ourselves and our problems and then, like we did after the breakup, it was all too late. Maybe that would have changed something if we had spoken out earlier. I don't know. Since the group 50+ Treff was said to be a kind of partner portal from the very beginning of my work for this group, it happened as it had to. It was a Friday before Pentecost in 2017, 8 years after Britta from Lower Austria had separated from me. We had a meeting there once again in a bar and its pub garden. I went there as usual with my friend Roman. Then came Pamela, a member of the 50+ Treff group and a year younger than me, and sat between Roman and me. In the course of the evening a one-off conversation developed between me and Pamela and we talked and laughed a lot, so that I didn't really notice the other participants anymore. In the process, I noticed that every time we had something to laugh about, she patted me on the upper arm or thigh. I registered well, but what now, because I wasn't the bravest in this regard. But I took my courage and asked her if we could not meet somewhere on Pentecost Saturday to go for a walk, which we also did the next day.

I fell out of the clouds and went to the community day of my community on Pentecost Sunday. But since it was always customary on days like this, after a short prayer, to talk about the path and one's own experiences with it, and that in front of about 20 people, of course voluntarily, I started after a while. As I said, I was 57 years old and had spoken to Pamela on the phone before entering the building. So, I said that I suffered from an incurable disease that could affect anyone and other flowery statements on my part. I looked around and except for distraught faces I couldn't really make out anything. What was I talking about? Well, of course there were questions and statements, such as: you are talking like a 16-year-old and one of those present, a 22-year-old student, asked me: Edi are you in love, which of course I couldn't deny. A month later, on July 15th, 2017, I imagined that Pamela and I were a couple, I went to see my son in Lower Austria for the last time, which I didn't know at the time. Since he soon realized that I was over-excited, I confessed to him that there was a new woman in my life and also showed him a picture of her, which I regretted afterwards. At that time, Pamela was already on a cure in Styria. When she came back, I found out that another member of the 50+ Treff group had followed her in this health resort and Pamela had taken me away. Since this man was not necessarily sociable either, this partnership between Georg and Pamela was only temporary. Well, there were more meetings and in August 2018 a meeting took place at a Heuriger in the 19th district. Some people in this group as well as I had started a group in Whatsapp and sent us back and forth photos all over the place. So, on this Friday, a new woman came into the group, named Anna, a native of Poland and nice to look at. She could laugh very heartily, which impressed me very much. She also joined our group in Whatsapp and then kept coming up with funny contributions, which gave this group a boost. One day in September 2017 she posted that the grapes in the 22nd district were ripe and that someone from this group could not help her with the grape harvest. She had earmarked a day for this the next weekend. The response to this was zero. So, I thought to myself, why not, go read grapes and make an appointment in the 22nd district. I really found a lot of grapes that we picked during the day and then processed into syrup and juice in the evening. But since nothing "ran away" on a Saturday evening, time passed and we became a couple that day. In mid-October, after a month of partnership, she said that she would feel more comfortable if she was left alone, which I had to accept. Good or not, that also broke up, but there were always meetings in the group and so in November 2017 in the 3rd district. There we were about 20 people, where we had some space problems in this restaurant. When the whole thing was over at around 9 am, we, Roman and I, went into the street where two women, named Tine and Julia, were standing. Suddenly Tine asked: What do we do now? I was a little perplexed because I hadn't expected such a question from a woman. Well, so we went to a nearby café and stayed there for about an hour. Then Tine found out that I was busy with computers and she said whether I could fix the problem with her computer at her home, which she assumed after giving her address in the 14th district. The woman was about two years older than me and not necessarily slim. This repair of the computer or this visit turned into more, although I didn't necessarily like it from the look. Most of the time I spent with her and with her. She had a new apartment, but apparently didn't really feel at home there, as far as I could tell, because she always had to go out to buy something or just to go somewhere, she was a passionate driver. During this time, she showered me with clothes and other things, and had always paid in the pub. When I asked her that I didn't want that, because I had enough clothes in my boxes in the meantime, she was a little nervous. So, one weekend she drove to her sister in deepest Burgenland and called from the car on the way there. For me, that was what broke the barrel. She had decided everything without consulting me and said that she could buy my love with heaps of gifts. So, this episode was over too. In the summer of 2018, Roman and I went dancing in the 1st district, both single, we had known the event for a long time and, above all, the two organizers. When we got there, there was almost no space left, so we both had to sit down at a table where two women were already sitting. One was called Graziella (partly Italian parents) and unfortunately, I don't remember the name of the second. Now that we were sitting at the same table, I also had to ask the ladies to dance and so

Graziella and I were soon sitting next to each other and she told me that she had problems with her PC. I knew the argument well by now and Graziella was a lot older than me, but still confirmed that I would see it at her home in the 16th district. There, too, it was the same result as with Tine, we came together. She had a long-term lease in the 17th district with a small house in the correspondingly large garden, where one could not move easily in front of a huge number of plants and trees. In addition, she had grapevines above the roof terrace, where we also harvested the grapes and then processed them, again an aha experience. Since it was not only possible to move around in the garden, this also applied to the interiors of the house and finally also to your apartment. The partnership was therefore limited in time. I myself am not exactly a fool of cleaning, but I would like to be able to move around in a room, I was cramped enough in 2012 anyway. At the beginning of November 2018, one Saturday morning after breakfast I left this connection in a hurry. I fell into a deep hole at this point as I had to wonder what I was doing wrong. 4 women and with everyone it didn't work out, was it my past, was it my "wealth"? Well, there was another dance event at the end of November a Saturday November 24th, 2018 My friend Roman persuaded me to go to this dance in the 2nd district. But I didn't feel like it. In the end, he finally got me that far. We sat at a table with about 8 people. Across from me I saw a blonde woman who, in my opinion, was in the company of an elderly gentleman. I hadn't danced very much that evening from 6 p.m. to 9 p.m. to live music. Towards the end, the lady in question came back to the table and said to Roman and me if we didn't want to dance there at all. I had only badly understood this statement and therefore did not react. Roman immediately jumped up and went dancing with her. Now this event was over and we went to the cloakroom. Suddenly this woman, named Ully, was standing next to me and asked: Are you going with me and by that, I mean Roman and me. After it was Saturday evening and not late either, I didn't mind going with me, and I told Roman that too. He also agreed and so after a long search about 8 people ended up in a bar in the 1st district. Before she went to the cloakroom, she gave Roman her cell phone number, which I only registered marginally. Well now we sat Ully next to me in this bar and Roman gave a lecture on shamanism and energetics. In the course of the evening, it turned out that Ully had not come with the elderly gentleman, but with her friend Monika. As soon as I registered this, I was a bit embarrassed, which I liked about the lady. Now Roman had her number, but I couldn't possibly ask for it. So, I took a business card from the restaurant and wrote my phone number on the back. When I left the restaurant, I gave her this card, which, unfortunately, Roman also noticed. So, I was in the devil's kitchen and Ully had two cell phone numbers from Roman and me. The next day, Sunday, I waited to see what was going on. Nothing happened in the morning, but at 2 o'clock the cell phone was and Ully was on the line. She asked me if we couldn't even go for a coffee. My answer to this: Immediately and immediately - you have a break in transmission. Yes, she still has to fix something and will call me back in about an hour. But it wasn't an hour, just a half-hour and we met in a coffee house in the 20th district. Then we went to the cinema there and because that wasn't enough, we also went to a lounge on the 1st floor. I told her, as I was used to it, everything about my past life, which may not necessarily be productive. Suddenly she turned to me and kissed me on the cheek. We have been a couple since then, even if there is a difference in age by a few years. Why? Because I believe she is the best of the 4 women before.

Neo-Catholic end

When I joined the fellowship or the path in 2011, it was clear from the start that it would take about 30 years to walk this path. Now in 2017 on this Pentecost weekend I had to make my experiences, what the interpretation of partnership on this way means and therefore I got a bit brooding. When my sister Maria from the community took her own life in April 2018, after 7 years of belonging, I decided to end the path and did the same in May 2018 at a Vespers for the deceased. My thought in this regard was that I could no longer agree with some arguments along the way. That applied of course to the interpretation of partnerships, as well as how to bring faith to life. Am I now a believer or not: This question cannot and I do not want to answer here, above all, can the individual individual himself? For my part I now try to live the faith after leaving the community. Since then, I have still been in contact with God, even if this is only expressed in silent prayers with him.

Customers

In the course of my life, I have certainly had several hundred customers whom I always treat with respect and courtesy, regardless of whether they are domestic or foreign. As for the customer base at the time I was selling newspapers and magazines, I have had several negative experiences. Since 99% of them were always foreigners, I didn't even have to look at my money, as the people had gone to their home country and ignored my demands. My customers, whom I am already completely different in the computer sector, are always happy when they call me. You know that I don't rest until the problem has been resolved and that can take time. But I don't remember a customer from the time I was creating software. This is a resident of Germany, but of a different parentage. His three companies include a dental practice, a dental laboratory and a dental depot. In the fall of 2010, his employee from the dental depot shop came to our shop. The background was that the calculation program no longer worked and he asked if I could fix it. Since this man did not necessarily have a commercial knowledge, I found that this program could no longer be saved. Now I had noticed that the whole thing basically consisted of three companies with a wide variety of approaches. Thus, as part of our company in the 20th district, we created an offer for all three companies with financial and inventory accounting, open item management. Customer and supplier call-off management and much more. I presented this to the boss and he began to accept individual parts of this offer and reject others. But since I always have the ambition to create everything 100%, that was also the case in this case, and of course also with regard to the fact that the decision was made to accept another part of our offer. But since software is not static, the program was often adapted. So, I went to his dental wholesaler up to four times a week to do this, each time for a thank you for seven years. Since the employees present there were not necessarily merchants, they could not carry out the annual inventory. That means until the inventory in 2017, this was carried out by me with the help of the people present there. But since I know from my commercial experience that something like this should be done within a maximum of two days, I had my difficulties in this regard. The last inventory was completed in stages within two weeks. It was agreed in advance that the invoice submitted by us would be paid three times. The first partial amount with a three-digit amount in euros has been paid, the rest is still open. The client's argument was that my program doesn't work, which is fundamentally contradicting itself. On the one hand, the software worked flawlessly for seven years and, on the other hand, they are still using it today and have also been using it for four years. So, we got back to a good 4-digit one. Even a letter from a lawyer threatening an order for payment went unheeded. Regarding my current customers, whom I look after as part of our business today, let me say that they are completely enthusiastic about me, because they know what they are getting from me. On the one hand, this is not just the prompt appointment, but also the customer's knowledge that I don't give up until I find a solution. It may well be that it takes time, but I am also happy every time I see that it works.

Résumé

You, as a reader, may now think that you have read this is no life. Yes, it might be, but as already mentioned, those were solely my decisions, whether they were right or wrong, can always only be determined in retrospect. So, the next question arises, whether I am happy. But since this is a purely subjective assessment, everyone would answer this differently. I am happy. Why? When I think about the time of my addiction, it wasn't really what is called life, so I'm glad I got through this period. How I managed that back then is still not clear, but I'm glad I got through that time. Whether I am satisfied, as I formulated it in my 1st book, remains unanswered. The reason for this is that my closest friend separated from me at his own request after a good 10 years, which I still don't understand to this day. I don't know what else life has prepared for me, but nothing more can actually come that would shake me.